Say Yes!

Say Yes!

Paula Morgan

Times
BOOKS

Library of Congress Cataloging in Publication Data

Morgan, Paula.
    Say yes!

    Poems.
    I. Title.
PS3563.087144S2   1977   811'.5'4   76-50827
ISBN 0-8129-0678-0

For Jonathan David
and
Lisa Beth

For my dear family and friends who
have weathered all the storms and have stayed
to applaud even when yours was the only
sound—I love you all.

And for the booksellers all over America
who were kind enough to put me on counters
and in windows; without
you nothing would have happened. Here we go again.

Paula Morgan

Contents

Me	3
Together	5
Lessons	7
Surprise	9
Marriage 1970s	11
My Son	12
Lisa Beth	13
An Ode to My Phone	14
Waiting	16
America's Hero	17
The Other Woman	18
Shrinks	20
Life	21
Rhea	26
My Mother	28
Making Rounds	29
Looking at Pictures	31
Saturday Father	32
An Ode to Bobby Short	34
The Great Middle Age Jewish Conspiracy	35
10 Minutes Terrific	37
You're On, Kid	40
Special Girl	41
Sleepless	43

$30 Haircut	45
Madmen	47
Fear No More	49
Stop	51
George C. Scott	54
That Girl	56
Power Thy Name Is Money	58
For Shepsie!	60
His Hand	62
Leonard	64
My Brother	65
No More Birthdays	66
25 Years	68
Elaine	70
Say Yes! Please!	71
Merry Go Round	72
The Pattern	73
What's Better?	75
Two Alones	77
The Man in the Dark Green Suit	79
Leah	80
There Are Hours	81
Amy	83
Gayle, Gayle	85

Hello! New Friend	87
Goodbye Take Care	88
Things	90
Dick	94
Salek	95
Cologne?	97
Where Do I Come From?	99
Rain	100
Sheila	102
Suicide	103
Nothing	105
Camp	106
Group Therapy	108
Theatre	110
Who Am I?	112
Maybe Tomorrow	115
Depressed	117
No Nos	118
Thursday	119
Mother's Day	122
Father's Day	124
Women's Lib—Yes or No	126
Television	128
Yellow Roses	131

Ask for all, but
expect nothing—only
the coming true of
your most impossible
dreams.

—Tennessee Williams

Say Yes!

Me

I never read the Koran
    smoked hash
    known EST
        or
    biofeedback
Or spent one minute
    contemplating
What I came in
    knowing
I never needed to
    learn
And what I could
    have used
No one ever taught
        Me
I'm not even street smart
I am a believer
I never think I'm being taken
'Tho' I know I am
There are days that my anxiety pounds
In my fist and sits on my chest so
Hard I can hardly breathe
There are days I am quite beautiful
And on a bad compulsive day
        Ugly
        Ugly

Every once in a while a special light
Shines on me for a moment
Just long enough to make me totally
Mad forever
      I am like you
      full of confidence and fear
      both at the same time
I want to survive—better and longer
And to do it with style
I have a love affair with life
      with my family
      and my friends
      and my kids—most of all
I am your mother
I am your lover
I am your child
I am a woman
      I am like you
      and we are
        the same!

Together

They came together
They were beautiful
Full of hope
Full of the stories of America, America
Gold in the streets

They came from
        pogroms—no Jews allowed
        ghettos' poverty—2000 years
        of living in one place—fear

They came from culture too—and music and a kind of
Arrogance
        they were the chosen
        they would endure
        they would survive
        they would succeed

It was hard. There was depression, war—a big war
        ovens, crematoriums, ghettos—only Jews allowed
        they survived
        they dreamed
        they fought
        they succeeded—Jews were now allowed

There was a country—a flag—there was an army,

and a new generation began
    they were still together
    they were old
    they were alive
    they were still together

How does that happen? This is 1977.

Lessons

What is there about us
We are not a moment like our
Mothers
    they married
    bore children and
    stayed with our fathers
    despite—
        forever
But We
    We love
    We marry
    We bear children
    and We search for
    new fathers for our children
    new ways to live
        over and over again
Our mothers
    tried so hard for us
    they said
    learn
    be free
    be strong
    have purpose

We did all that
　　　But We
　　　　　didn't learn patience
　　　　　　　or
　　　　　　　forgiveness
　　　　We
　　　　　didn't learn
　　　　　how to make it work
　　　　We are not our mothers
So here We are
　　　　brilliant
　　　　sophisticated
We know everything
　　　　We stand at our windows
　　　　night turning to day
　　　　a lifetime gone
　　　　　and how do We stand?
　　　　　We stand alone!

Surprise

The ballroom was huge. It was the most beautiful gold room
I'd ever seen
A princess in a palace
It was a Monday
We were in love
It was my birthday
It was New York.

The band began to play and we danced and whirled and
It was a glorious surprise, he had asked the hotel to fix the
Room and hired the band. Just for us, just we two.
He was Gilbert Roland, and I was Mata Hari
Lalique glasses and French champagne
      And streamers, all colors
      And the 2 of us.

There was a box from Tiffany's all wrapped in grey velvet
A hansom cab down 5th Avenue . . . I was Gloria
Swanson and Garbo and God—he was—well . . . he was

And time came and days passed and the streamers were
Hung for someone else and the hansom cab was hired by
   another
Couple who took another ride down 5th Avenue
And I cried

And I cried
And I bought two hats
And I went to Ardens
And I looked
And I looked
He was gone forever.

And then a friend came, and I saw Ethel Merman sing, "Roses
Turn" in *Gypsy*
And I kept the box
And I lost the man
And I never saw him again—except in my head
And I never forgot the ballroom.

I keep looking for it.

Marriage 1970s

Now, what is marriage anyway?
I always thought it was Dorothy Maguire and Robert Young in
Claudia.
And when I found out it wasn't, well, a sadness
Came into my tower.
The part of the wife was always played by Ruth Hussey.
(Now who wants to be Ruth Hussey, except Ruth Hussey)
The other woman was Carole Lombard   of course,
That's better.
So marriage was Carole Lombard at Bonwits
Being pursued by a misunderstood husband
And his little girl loved "them" and hated her mean mama
Who was big in charities, and smoked and was never home.
He couldn't get a divorce—and Carole was too good to
Be kept

That's what marriage was, either Ruth Hussey or Dorothy
Maguire—but, never, Carole Lombard. The other alternatives
were
>   1. Married and bored
>   2. Being alone
>   3. Being kept
>   4. Raising children alone and being kept
>   5. Or remarrying, raising children alone and
>   helping to keep your husband
It's 1977
And only the names have been changed. The alternatives are
The same, only with more bravado and we're all alone anyway
>   Maybe I should get a job at Bonwits

11

My Son

My son used to ask me how he was born and I have always
Told the same story—
I asked for a friend.
I asked God for a special child—a child with blue eyes
And a wide smile and my very, very own
      And God listened
      And he was born
      And I was never lonely again
Now he is older and he knows how he was born
But my reasons are even stronger now
He is all I could want
He is filled with energy, and curiosity, and eyes
That fill with tears when hard truths come
      He is an enormous joy
      He is a reason for believing in life and birth and truth
Please, my son. Don't be different. Don't let the world change
What you are . . . I couldn't stand it.
You are still not just a son. But the friend I asked for . . .
      Maybe there is a God!

Lisa Beth

Lisa Beth—
　　My survivor
How are you
How are you
　　　You came from pain
　　　You came from love
　　　You came when a marriage was over
　　　You are terrific
　　　You were so small
　　　I could hardly breathe every time
　　　I looked at you
　　　So glad you came
　　　You have given me so much strength
　　　I look at you and I am the world
　　　You were so needed
　　　A mother needs a daughter
　　　I love your face
　　　I Love You
　　　You have made it all worthwhile

　　　You are a survivor
　　　You are mine
　　　You Are Me!

An Ode to My Phone

My telephone
    is really everything!
It is life's exercise
So much happens on it!
    I cannot live without it
    It is my truest friend.
Where else can you hear everything
You'll ever need to know about—anything—
    In an instant!
I cannot even think of any form of life without it
What do people do—stranded—
    No telephone!
Darwin would've had a telephone theory
Who will ever forget "smiling Don Ameche"
    And pale Loretta Young
    And their story
    My God
    How gorgeous.
You may call me anything you like
    But call me!
Leave me alone—forever—
But ... give me a good, clean telephone
And ... I am again, revived, reborn, alive.

Can I give it a medal
Can I kiss it? No . . . but
I can tell you—anything—everything—
With my 'phone.
Just think of . . . Martha Mitchell, Louella, and Hedda,
Joan, and Clare Booth Luce,
      Without a 'phone—
      That we cannot do without
         forever and ever
                Amen!

Waiting

—So glad you came
  your pictures
  are terrific
—I mean this is a great shot

—Your reading
  was really great
  we hope we'll
  be able to use you
—You look marvelous
—Now, don't call us,
  we'll call you

I waited
And I waited
They Never
              Called

America's Hero

He hated graft, McCarthy, and Fascism
He loved Scotch, cigarettes, and brains
America, the great middle west,
And being a celebrity
His voice said "This is London"
And the world stopped and listened

He said hello to me—and I stopped
It was a long hello—he never said goodbye
It was "goodnight and good luck"

He was Ed Murrow
And I was never the
same again.

The Other Woman

The other woman
       sleeps till 12:00
       takes 3 hours to dress
       doesn't jump out of the shower
       to get a bottle,
       or change a pair of pants
       because
       she is childless.

The other woman
       is . . . kind, sweet, loving, and,
       never has a headache,
       because
       She doesn't have a head.
       She is always calm, serene, smiling
       she can tell your husband, as she mixes a martini
       that he is marvelous
       because
       she's never lived with him, yet
       She smells of "joy"
       she is seductive
       she wears new lingerie
       she even has a clean purse—without cookie crumbs
       because
       she has only . . . herself.

I have more than myself—I am very busy !
If I ever had 3 minutes
      I could smell of "joy"
      I could wear white pants, and be seductive.
If he wants her,
good luck to them both
      she is a bore
      she is a clean, new toy
      (how lucky can you be)
I know—I'm a real *woman*
      part mother
      part toy
      and a lot of person
      if that's not enough
Goodbye.

Shrinks

In my group everyone who is anyone has one

Now, first you have your own
Then your husband (if you have one), has one
Your kids, then, have theirs—individually, of course
Then, there are group plans (like an airline ticket sale)

Now, can you imagine the dough these people are making?
Is it really helpful, does it work, anyway, it takes
a lot of time, it's great conversation and it is deductible
—if you can prove to the I.R.S. that you really need it
Now, that can be damaging, maybe later, depending
On what schools your kids plan to attend, if any

Shrinks really are similar—thoughtful, elegant, cool,
detached, and r-i-c-h—and they l-i-s-t-e-n.
I have a cousin who was, and is, a holy terror, and he's
the high priest of Bedford Drive, it's because he has
John L. Lewis Eyebrows, and smokes a pipe—l-i-s-t-e-n-s.

All this money to learn to enjoy a hot dog?

Life

Laughing
 Running
 Jumping
 Crying
  Not thinking
  Just doing
 Small-sized persons
  Living every moment
 Hanging from bars
 Standing on heads
 Bodies stretching
 Shouting
  Childhood—
   Marvelous
  Adolescence—
   Difficult
   Minds sharp
   Silly
   Angry
Not men yet, but not children anymore
  Important time
  Then high school—
 Medium-sized people
  Thoughtful
  Carrying books
  Grumbling

Screaming,
Tests, points, papers
Dirty tennis shoes
Beautiful skirts
Long hair
Funny jeans
Thinking, doing, preparing
College
Driving
Drinking
Smoking
Thinking
Term papers
Lectures
The Future
Credits
Units
Tuition
The wrong girl
The right boy
Theosophy
Marches
Protests
Degrees
Speeches

The Future
Graduate school
  A practice
  Money
    Or lack of it
  Worry
    Today is tuff
  Study
  Work
  Think a lot
  Dream a little
    Work, work, work
  Quiet
    The Future
  When will it come
Marriage—
  The rat race
  Baby coming
  Mortgages
    Work, save
  Banks, loans
  Taxes
    Fear
Body not stretching, not like before
A quiet shouting, inside

Is this what it's
   All about?
Children growing
Age coming—age is here damn it
Dreams
   Some succeed
   Some not
Questions—
      Maybe to drop out
   Is this what I did all of
   That for
      Is this what I
      Wanted
         Questions
         Discontent
         Boredom
Remembering—
   That playground
   and
   A childhood
      to
   Prepare me
For what?
   To get old
   and
   Tired

But
Did I do
What I
Thought I would
and
Did I become
What I wanted
and
With whom
Or was I so told how to live that
I never had a chance
To just do
and
Just be
and
Now it's too late
The voyage here is almost over and
I can remember pieces of
What was once
My memory has begun to fail now
And I guess
So have I
But then
So have we all
Is that all there Is?

Rhea

Rhea is an original
I mean with whom you can share
       lox and cream cheese
       or go to Loehmann's
Rhea is abrasive
       Intolerant
       Opinionated
       Hostile
       And quite horrible
       Who would go to all the trouble of
       going to the hall of records
       to find out exactly how old I am—you know the kind
       We all have one!
We met when all the laughter had left me and
She stayed to keep me laughing so hard
I forgot my pain
       With this lady
         You can steal
         Forge a prescription
         Maybe even discuss the Talmud
I guess she's part of my life, damn it—the
part I'd like to forget—and
       somehow keep remembering

Don't we all need someone
to make sure our feet are
never off the ground!
Everyone does—
It's part of being human
Having
an insulting
difficult
simply marvelous
ego-stripping
Friend

My Mother

She is a paisley shawl
        a black jet tiara
        and the Eyes of all the Jewish Martyrs
She never played Pan, belonged to the P.T.A.
        drove a car pool, or baked cookies
She did take us early to opera and lectures and concerts
        Culture ... culture ... culture ...!
She is the original believer
        In women's rights
        Abortion
        Birth control
        Divorce
She believes in Me.
She is the atypical Jewish Mother
        She is a child of Europe
        She could never be called an immigrant
        Though she was
She is a Lady
She is My Mother. She cares in Her own way
        I care in Mine

Making Rounds

I look back on all that
Wondering *how* I did it
I know *why*
>   I wanted that gold ring
>   I wanted the star on that door
>   I wanted the applause
And for that
>   I preened
>   I dieted
>   I studied
>   I walked—oh! I walked
I spent the madness of my youth
Asking strangers to tell me I was special
Asking a world to take me in that wanted to keep me out
I wanted all of that rejection
I needed all of that acceptance
>   And I was not alone
>   A whole city seemed caught up
>   And was
Oh! I got a piece of that ring
I got a bit of star
>   Was it enough
>   Was it worth all of that
>   Pain?

I don't know worth
I do know love
    Yes! for me
    It was what I had to do
    It was all I knew then
    I don't know much more now
I know it is a time to remember
That adventure
The real time of my growing
    up!

Looking at Pictures

Looking at pictures is a mistake
Today I look awful
    In the pictures I look great
Today every line shows
    In the pictures it's always beauty, color and smiling
Today is bleak
    and empty
Yesterday looks so terrific
Better than it was in kodachrome
Better than it was in ektachrome
    Better than it can be in life
    Now, what will tomorrow be
    If yesterday was beautiful
    And today is cold
    What is tomorrow
    Can it be worse than today?
Emile Coué said "Every day and every way
we get better and better"
    To be a Christian Scientist and believe that.

Saturday Father

We once loved
We fought
Oh, how we fought.
We once loved
And then it died
There was no more fight, or hate, or anxiety
There was emptiness.

Now he comes . . . and he loves them . . . as best he can,
And he buys toys and games, and hamburgers, and they wait
To see him and be with him.
          and He tried
          and I hoped
          and It died
We share nothing, neither time, nor friends, nor
Experience, nor even laughter
His feelings for me are guarded, and empty, and angry
          A quiet anger.

His going and coming used to be terrible. Not any more
It's almost a relief. How does that happen
          That once we loved
          Then we died?
It's the years of the lack of care, the lack of sharing.
I wonder what will become of him . . . he seems such a
Wanderer . . . he answers nothing, he asks nothing, he seems
To want nothing.

But I am a woman
Who lived with a man
And loved a man
And bore him children
And believed in dreams
I thought we would fight forever.
But now I have given up, there is really nothing left.
Even my hope for what could have been is gone—not
for anything I can name, but everything I can't
Name, or can't feel.

I am a woman
And he is a man
But we did love
And tho' It died
And It cannot be
I did feel once that I cared
Perhaps those moments are what love is

It would be a miracle to start again, to forget all
The empty yesterdays, but
He would have to look at me, and see me, and know me
And he won't. Maybe he can't. It's too bad.

I am a woman
Who loved a man
Indeed
I did. I did.

An Ode to Bobby Short

"Let there be you"
      Dear man
"Let there be me."
        You were my
introduction to
      Rogers and Hart
      Mabel Mercer
       and
      What was left of the Cotton Club.
When you took me home one night
A man in blue
Said Hey! do you live here
If you don't you don't belong
And I remember I said you belonged to me
And the man in blue walked away
      You continue to give me joy
And I continue to believe that you
Belong to me
      And so does everyone who has ever heard you!

The Great Middle-Age
Jewish Conspiracy

You're supposed to be married no matter what
You're supposed to have children who aren't just
    children
    But super achievers
    Inventors, doctors, lawyers, rich ... rich
You're supposed to be pretty, wear a size 10, and cope.

Now it doesn't really matter if you have colitis, an ulcer,
And you really don't like your husband.
We are super women, we are great, we cope.
Do we ... do we ever ...

We support every medium, fat doctor, astrologer, psychiatrist,
Plastic surgeon from here to Long Beach.
We are not found in bars, or hotel rooms but at macrame
Sessions— understand your whole potential—
At lunch for Reiss Davis, U.J.A., bonds for Israel, exceptional
children, spastic children, gifted children, O.R.T., Hadassah,
Etc. Etc. and So Forth.
Most of my ladies live in their cars. It's called
Mommy's limousine service, to lessons, lessons, lessons
But what happened to the graduates of Bennington and
    Columbia
and Bryn Mawr? Are we fulfilled?

Are the marriages great—and romantic—and rewarding—
  Or is time going
  And dreams passing
  And age coming
  And husabnds waning
  Is it really worth it—is there a way out?
What if I'm not home, or he misses his lesson
When did I last walk down La Cienega romantically
With someone, anyone
When did I not worry about rashes and flat feet and
  Braces and school
Why not run away, run away . . . and dream of
  Just dream
How would they be without me—I don't know.

  I am responsible
  I am Jewish
  I have super achievers
  I wear a size 10
  I have a waning husband
   And I cope
   Oh! I cope
    Isn't that terrific

10 Minutes Terrific

I saw him
Standing alone
    White pants
    Yellow windbreaker
    Black hair
    A pipe
I had never seen
    him before
maybe
    a hundred times
I was alone
We looked
My mind said
Forget it
    He'll have a wife
      or he had a wife
He sees his kids on Sunday
    If I look back
    because he's cute
It will all start
Again
The love
The pain
And the anger

Is it better for
          10 Minutes Terrific
          To have love
          Pain
          Anger
To start again
I don't know
I'm too scared
I got up
I started walking to
          the door
The room was very
          noisy
But, for an instant
          our eyes met
I stopped
I looked at him

My, my—he looked at me
We said nothing
We both know
        it was pow
        For 10 Minutes

        Terrific

        It Seemed Not Worth It—
            Am I Wrong

You're On, Kid

For Myself

It only takes a moment
    For all the yesterdays and their pains
    To go away with those words,
      "you're on, kid"
    all of a moment you can feel your face
    light up and that candle in your soul
    burning
    you just lost 30 pounds
      you dropped 10 years
      suddenly grew 5 inches
    And it didn't even take a sentence—just three words
      that heat is flowing inside
      when the audience says
        I love you
    To feel that way by yourself, without an audience
    that would be—marvelous
    but that's not possible—is it?
    the lights
    the camera
    the great smell of pancake
Heaven
    who said it's for nothing
      it's for
          everything!

Special Girl

When I was 5
>   he walked into my measles bedroom ... in his
>   black tuxedo ... young ... my face filled
>   with calamine ... and kissed me

When I was 8
>   my mother was in Europe
>   He took me to Bullock's Wilshire, bought me a
>   blue coat trimmed in velvet, and took me to
>   Perino's to lunch
>   and told me I was his special girl

When I was 14
>   He took me to N.Y., told me there's a great
>   world out there, took me to Saks, bought me
>   a suit from London and told me I was pretty
>   and I believed it

When I was 17
>   He said, o.k., you want to be an actress
>   so, go be
>   but you have a contract with me
>   and I was on my way

He came to all the openings
He was there at all the closings
He told me I was swell, no matter what.
When everything around me said,

>   "No"!

He said,

>   "Yes"!

He said they are fools—they don't know.
When I married someone he wasn't sure of, and had my son
He said, I'll help you, and he did
When I had my baby girl, and the marriage was finished
He said, you're O.K. by me,
When I said, marriage and I are not compatible
He yelled, but he said, O.K.
I want to make him know somehow
        That no matter what happens next
        I walk very tall
        I can really handle everything
I believe I can because he believes in me
        and it sure helps, doesn't it.

Sleepless

Who are all the people in the picture-perfect houses
Who can turn out the lights and fall asleep
They must have beautiful bedrooms ... beautiful lives ...
    and beautiful husbands
I have none of these
But in my house live beautiful people—in faded chairs
    that need redoing
But very bright lives
So why can't I sleep
It's because I'm lonely
Lonely for someone to buy pretty sheets for
Or a new nightie
Or even share the late show
Well! ... it's not going to happen tonight
So, I'd better stop thinking
And look again at my beautiful people
And tell myself maybe tomorrow—
And try and sleep

Someone asked me if I am ever lonely
I always say, No! ... No!
    I'm fine
    I am a liar
I don't dare let myself remember I am lonely
Or I'll crack
And I don't like that

I only remember I am fine
I am always fine no matter what
Who are all those pretty people
Who fall asleep as soon as the lights go out and never stare
          at the dark
Are they a special form of human?
They must be
Everyone I know is like me
Oh! there goes the phone
Someone else who can't sleep
Hello! . . . Hello!
Wrong number
I'm getting tired now
It's almost morning

Thank God, and Seconal

Good Night.

$30 Haircut

You know
        that feeling
something
        marvelous
        will happen
You stand in
the mirror
        all the colors
            in place
        looking at yourself
A minute ago
        I looked rather
        awful
And at this moment
        all the age
            has gone away
Can't a good girdle
        and a $30 Haircut
            do wonders
Tonight
        I'm going to hear Sinatra
        Here I am a middle-aged
        bobby-soxer getting ready
            to swoon
Is it to relive my youth
        Was it all that wonderful?

And since
        I'm the only one around my answer
        must be Yes
No one will know I'm there
But I will, and for an instant
        I've forgotten all the
        pain
        All that
        time
I'm a bobby-soxer all over again
        Not wiser
        Not older
        but young
                and
        free
                and . . .
That impossible time
        The clock has stopped
        and I am new
        all new
        With only the regrets in my head
        not my face
Yeah, a $30 Haircut is a miracle.

Madmen

I used to think
madmen were
concentrated armies
     or
movements
     or
causes—
I used to be a child
I'm not anymore
    now
Madmen everywhere
stopping us from feeling
    bombs everywhere
    lockers and planes
There's no place to run anymore
What does a mother
tell her children
Who read it—and see it?
on the tube
Not the Viet war dead or
The Korean plane count or
How many were gassed at Treblinka
But our own streets
what happened to that world
where we stayed
innocent forever?

My fear of death
for those I love
is all too close now
Anxiety sits in my chest
   waiting
We wake up every day so shocked
we no longer
assume that man
has passed through
the dark ages! We know he has not
Is there no end
We must just try and live
and not think
Maybe our turn
   won't come!
Maybe it will go away
like a bad dream
   "Somewhere
    Over the Rainbow."

Fear No More

She held his
    hand so tightly
    joyful, excited
    frightened, but
    secure
She was in the
    ocean
    for the first
    time, and he
    was showing
    her how
He told her
the ocean was
her friend
She believed him
She screamed
    with laughter
She screamed
    with joy
He turned to me
    waiting and
    watching on
    the shore
and said
    O.K. Ma

And as I watched them
            together
                The waves
                lightly brushing
                them
            I could feel
            my beach robe
            wet
                not with
                the ocean
            but with a mother's
            happy tears
They are
            happy, he is
            helping her
            learn the
                world
                I have
            taught him
            well—he
            has learned
            all the lessons
He will help her
He will hold her hand
                I was very
                    happy.

Stop

They say it is
      better than Auschwitz.
      is it?
They say we show the
world our strength
      do we?
They say we fight
we are not afraid
we are Jews
we will survive
      will we?
Cannot a voice
      a voice of reason
a mother's pain
a bloody face
a tank blown in bits.
Does it matter
      whose?
Does it matter
whose son fell first?
They are too young
      to die
it is all wrong
Does no one hear
      the anguish
        of the mothers

Who bear the sons—
who must bury
            them too—
Is all reason
            gone
Is oil, my son,
more important than
you are?

You are more worthy,
you are part of me,
I die when you die
            stop
            stop
The price is too much
I cannot endure
the suffering
            —and if we
        win
The lines of
boxes will never
            stop

Someone listen
        we are burying
        our sons—

Life is no
        longer worth
        anything—
            is it?
If life is
        worth nothing,
        and death is
        without honor—
        then what is
        it all about?
            Someone listen.
And stop this madness.

        we beg you

George C. Scott

There is a conspiracy in this country
That men are unromantic
Rather dull
Aggressive
Money wanters
Moneymakers
Money spenders.
Now, let us discuss George C. Scott.
I was not a fan of General Patton
—Or of any military man
But, George C. Scott in *Petulia*
With his broken nose, spindly legs, neck like a truck driver,
And, in his shorts
Well
He is a man!
He made me forget poems, prose, and my intellect.
I mean he was, and is, gorgeous
He is midwestern, an actor, much married
But *gevalt*—I'd change it all
All my middle-class ideologies about men
With that beast—Scott—
I notice Coleen Dewhurst married him twice!
Now marriage is not my favorite
But you can't lose too much with him—I mean really—
I notice Julie Christie has never been the same

I'd even start saluting the flag
    For
        George C.
            And that's a lot
                For even Scott!

That Girl

It sometimes flashes through
I see that girl
    walking up that sidewalk
in New York
    everything moving
      so much
        excitement
        energy and
          confidence.
I see that girl
    And when I do—I sometimes wonder
what happened to her
Did she really have
All of that energy
    or was it New York's
      special amphetamine?
      And did all that hope
go away with the years?
    Did it get watered down?
    Did she get acceptable
and grown up?
I look at her in my mind's eye
and I think wow!

You thought you had it all
Your way didn't you kid
It was going to be
Saturday night forever
          and you could get in and out
of everything
couldn't you?
I think I'll leave you in my head
where I find you
          Even if I met you now I'd
             look at you and say
How lucky you are
Such passion for life !
I wonder if you knew kid
that the sidewalk
you walked was not
the yellow brick road.
No! it was only a sidewalk
But when next we meet
          I'm not going to tell you.
I want you to remember it
          as only you can
          Because you're very special
You're my youth.

Power Thy Name Is Money

I came face up today
to the power structure
    in a building like a mausoleum
    with a desk full of Tiffany ashtrays
and Steuben Glass, immaculate and orderly
There sat a man who can control peoples' lives
He was not a man
    not anymore!
A man has soul
    This man was
a super-oiled, plastic-based, well-made
    machine
His eyes were not blue, no, the color of steel
    As I looked at him I realized
he really had nothing
Only what his money could buy
And I wondered how much love had been bought today
    Kafka was right, he was the
    man who had become the machine
      and I don't know how to talk to
      a machine
      never again will I try

How dreadful to have all that power unless
it gives joy and love. And if I ever thought
I'd like some
      No! No! God,
       Listen
No power, please—
I met a man without a soul today and I will
never forget it!
      Soul is one luxury
      I can afford.

For Shepsie!

Our dialogue consists of
1. "What's there to eat?"
2. "I need to go to the library"
3. "Make an appointment with the dentist"
4. "Do you know about hypnosis?"
5. "Don't bother me"
6. "Finals this week"
   "I said close the door"
That beautiful baby boy
   is now an adolescent
You know what that means
It means—involved with self
All the social amenities are gone
   It's all growing
   and glands moving
   But he's very interesting
    when I do see him
   He's brimming with
    Anger
    Ideas
    Energy
    Curiosity
Books say if you live through this
   Well! I got through all the rest
   But this one
    is a test

It's not terrible yet
But it's on the way
      Please adolescence
         hurry—and go away
         I'm not young enough
to go through all that
        Is that what age appropriate means
        Well!
            Mine isn't!
There are moments
when I see the man
you are going to be
        It fills me with so much joy, and wonder
How lucky to be
        Your Mother.

His Hand

For Zayde

I remember his hand
    all freckled
    old, plump
       and in mine
He was a Hasid
And on Yom Kippur
as he prayed in that old shul as if Yom Kippur were his
      his white beard and black coat
      that look of him
      his concentration on his God
      the wisdom of the sages
      I would wave at him from the window but he would
      eye me sharply
He had many children and grandchildren
But I was his favorite
As I got older and started
questioning his God
      he even tolerated that!
When it was time for him to go, and the angel Gabriel
had called, it was very late, he was ready

He gave me his hand
His hand was in mine until that last
moment
I will never forget that feeling
as I write now I can see it—his hand
all
freckled
plump
and
warm
and in mine.

Leonard

Your life has order
      mine has not.
Your life is yours alone
      and mine is not.
You seem hard and invulnerable
while everything about me is open,
      like a huge trunk for anyone to see.
You are close-mouthed,
and yourself.
How are we friends? It was so long ago
at the St. Regis.
Our first date lasted twelve hours—my—
Yet, you have never loved me.
that has always bothered me.
      I cannot find you out
      and I have stopped trying.
You have always protected me,
been both cynical and kind.
It is a badge of honor to have you as my friend.
How I smile when I think of our days in the saloons
      and how many times you have bailed me out
      when I had nowhere to turn.
I hope I have brought you joy.
I know—I am a headache,
      and of everyone I have ever known
      I would trust you with my life.

My Brother–I'm Sorry Jerry

When I was little, I thought he was everything.
When I got bigger he was every intellectual proletarian hero
I thought he was a world saver
An idealist
A thinker
He spoke with big words, and had red books
His books were red, very red
And so were his thoughts
And he married the wrong
girl, and I was
sad.
The first real disappointment
Do we ever get over that, ever? No matter how many
joys may follow. Never. Never.
It's a locked, unspoken pain. It's a teacher to start guarding
your heart

I hate it.
I love him still.
My brother.

No More Birthdays

What is a birthday?
For our children
it seems they have passed
another stage of life and time
and it is so festive
Their life is a huge balloon
       Happy Birthday!
I want not to be remembered
a day older than maybe yesterday
It's an indignity
to give a woman a party
at 40
       Why advertise
       that the trip is nearly over?
We should start a movement
       Girl children have
       parties 'til 21
       Boy babies
       maybe 30
       That's enough
I have forgotten my birthday
       And I'm sure my mother
       will never tell
       If she did
       she'd lie

If I get to a hundred
            maybe then
But until then
            the candles are
            for the children
I hate that commercial
            "I'm not getting older,
            I'm getting better"
Better for what?
Dietrich says
            "A woman that will tell her age
            will tell anything" and I wouldn't
            want to argue with her
Am I afraid of age?
            Isn't everybody?
                    Amen

25 Years

The anniversary is supposed to celebrate
25 years of togetherness
      Now what does that mean?
      I mean in light years
         It means about four wars
         The kids get grown and go away
         The chairs get redone many times
         You buy a lot of season tickets
         By that time
which means all communication has stopped
         (we talk between acts now)
You start thinking about lifting your face
And when you finally get that trip to Europe
to visit the graves of the greats,
your husband says "it's cold—let's
get out of here"
And it is really cold—everywhere!

25 years
And the trip you worked so hard for
is such a bore
Now Hallmark may bomb me
But I think we should take a personal vote
        and abolish anniversary, forget time
after all
        25 years is totally enough,
            don't you think
We served our time
Now
let's serve ourselves
a slice of truth
Let's have a day that is honest
really honest
That's the best anniversary
        And anyway you are still my friend.

Elaine

It's about that time of the year
It seems a moment ago
I knew nothing about death till you died
I don't know anything about it now
One minute we were laughing
The next minute you weren't
I see you all the time
In my mind's eye
Smiling, and laughing smoking Pall Malls in your big red car
And shouting "hurry . . . hurry"
I miss you
Everyone does
You left too soon
There was more of life to do
The time we had was precious and fun
I think somehow—you know—I think of you and always will
You haven't really gone
You wouldn't do that
Without telling me first.

Say Yes! Please!

I look back—
        because when the swells happen it's
        impossible to stop and register it all
        When it all stops then I can reflect
I forget sometimes how many no's I've heard—
        how many tears I have shed—when the no's
        came always, at the worst time or for the
        best things
Sometimes I forget and just remember the good
It's easier
I never thought pain was necessary to build
        my character
        only my character lines
I always thought acceptance was the best
        and it is—I want all little children to have
        instant acceptance, so that twenty years later
        they won't have to spend their lives on black
        leather couches talking to a special form of human
        called a shrink—who really can't fix it anyway—
Not without our help !
No one can
Only ourselves
        Say Yes!
            Please!

The Merry-Go-Round

Don't you love the merry-go-round?
Don't you love to catch the brass ring?
Even when you know it's only brass
I love to spin, go up and down
Listening to the music
'Round and 'round, never stopping
My merry-go-round stopped . . .
And I got off
The brass ring turned black so fast
I forgot that it was ever gold

Someone said it was time to get off
Someone said find something real
It's better for you
Is it? I loved the ride, I could have gone
On forever and never would have known the
Difference . . . would I?
      I did love the ride . . . I hope I won't be sorry

Why did I ever listen to that someone
I did love that ride.

The Pattern

For Gussie

There is something
wrong
Something wrong with
        the pattern
                I mean life and death
We pass through
        all that beginning
when we are young
        and beautiful
Strong enough
        to fight for
                money and identity
And just when
we can finally finally stop
        All of our fighting
        age comes
        Then sickness
        and the game
        is all over
Everything we are
Everything we've learned
Gone
        into a box
                Finished

And it took
such a short time
There must be a
        way to do it
that it lasts longer
That the longer is
        better
            That it doesn't
            end with a
            few tears and
            a damned box
The pattern is all wrong
There must be
something we don't
know
        Somewhere
        maybe
Shangri-La
In the Valley of
the Blue Moon
        James Hilton
        You knew
        Didn't you.

What's Better?

If sex was better than
        almond rocca
If sex was better than
        lox and cream cheese,
now that it's all so free and accessible,
Then why do millions keep running madly to
        "Weight Watchers"
        "Be Thin"
        Diet Doctors
        Diet Pills
        Diet Shots
Well, doesn't that tell us something? It does me
I must tell you
        Masters and Johnson never asked me anything
        Kinsey was confused
        and Freud was misguided.
Every mother knows
        Cocoa calms the nerves
        Rice takes care of the stomach
        And chicken soup can cure anything
Then our conclusion must be that food is
        terrific
        That sex is questionable
        And if you have a choice—

If it were my last day
    I'd spend it eating
      Wouldn't you?
Now, let me decide what
    and where
    so I can
    plan
    ahead
    when that
    day comes
     Listen,
     without
     it being
     my last
     day,
      I could
      start
      right
      now
Couldn't You?

Two Alones

I am so jealous of
    Those couples
    in their jeans
    and boots
    walking together
    so close
Walking down tiny streets
    smiling
Looking into windows
    small interesting windows
    and
    talking to each other
    really talking
That always stuns me
They seem as if they care
that whole look of them
Nothing in their pasts
to guard them
against being free with one another
    How did we go away so fast?
The old jeans almost fit
but the texture of us
is not the same
We hold hands
and look into windows
not really speaking!

77

Not really looking, into each other
        but just those windows
Anything outside is better than
        to stop
          and
        ache
          for what
          is no longer
          part of
          us!
Why do we live this way
Is it easier?
holding hands and
not really holding hands
is holding no one
So
        here we are
Two alones
        walking together
        Time passing
        Years lost
I hate the picture
        He must too

A Man in a
Dark Green Suit

Why do we choose
what we choose
He was tall, and his eyes were blue, and there was something
    in his walk
A laugh, human
A special way of looking at things
A special way of looking at me.

He was safe
        And we did love
        We did, we did.
        Will we again?
        Does anything ever end!

Time has not changed the color of his eyes—but
the way he looks at me is not the same.
He does not laugh any more!
The years have not been kind to him—
        Does he love someone else
        Does he love himself
Will he ever be the same again?
Questions . . . that cannot be answered. Maybe
it's better not to ask. But, I wonder. I wonder.
He was awfully cute in the dark green suit.

Leah

Her face was
      patrician
Her walk
      tall and straight
      She was well boned
        and well born
I always thought she
      belonged to live
      at a different
      time
Her name was Leah
She was not like other grandmothers
      She wore chiffon
      in the kitchen and she spoke of things
      alien to her generation
I don't know if she believed
all that religious tradition
      She did adore me and I thought
      she was a queen
      She did not live to see my children
      She would have liked what she would have seen
      In her world that had seen so much tragedy
      she was a heroine
I wonder if much of what she was didn't rub
off on me
      No! I just stopped wondering
        I know it did!

There Are Hours

Sometimes
when baby is asleep
My son gone
House quiet
2 hard hours
    —I drink the wine
     I eat the food
    —Watch the news alone
The day was fine, so much to do
But the nights
    —one is fine
    —some are not
    —some nights don't matter
    —people call
    —no one matters
    —no one I want
     no one I need
    —no one who matters
Will it ever matter?
    —another wine
    —is this why people drink?
    —I could answer
I don't

I could be high on
    a fellow
I say no
    I don't know why
This is my time
If anything mattered
    I'd answer
Oh! finally
    a sound
    The two hours
    must have passed
    Baby's up—
    The phone rang
    it's my son
The empty space
    is over for now
    Do you have any
    empty space
    Doesn't everybody

Amy

I see you in your blue
coverall
age 2
      blonde curls
and little ivory face
      different
At 11
you wore funny jeans
and you were nature's child
      eager
      shy, falling
      over yourself like a puppy
I have always watched you
      Your aloneness
      And that temper
      And your poetry
      too timid to tell it
      or show it
But I have heard much
      of what you write
      And I know who you are
      I only hope you do
Yesterday, still at 15
      blonde and
      with that ivory face
      but almost a woman

A thrill rushed onto
    me—Amy
    I can't see that woman
    that you are finding in you
I want only to see the
    child in
    the coverall
    and to
    beg you
    to stay
      no matter what the pain
    Different from the others
      because
      you are

Gayle, Gayle

You are the earth mother
Tho' you must believe in fantasy
    if you believe in me
Behind your eyes I see
    mostly clouds
The smile does not give you away
    But the eyes,
    Do I read right?
I always thought
happiness is
exactly what you have
    if not you
then who of us could claim that?
    I would call on you for anything
But to whom do you call?
And when you need
who bathes your need in love
    The children
    The husband
    Really,
    Who?
Questions I should not ask
I have
    You never answer
because
    "no answer is also an answer"

And you are not the only one like you
You arc one of many friends
who bury their yearnings,
      put them away
      for later. When does later come?
      No,
         please,
            don't
            don't answer
I want not to know
      and so do you.

Hello! New Friend

Hello! new friend
    You had a special sound
    that made me feel
    my madness was
    welcome
    And even tho' we'd never met—you
    were not a mystery
I who fright easily
and cover it with noise
    suddenly,
        when we did meet
    I knew I had nothing
        to cover
    You seem kind
    and sensitive to my
    fear of losing
        what has taken a lifetime
        for me to grasp
    And I have found
    something special
        not just
        for today
    but for all the new tomorrows
    We'll need to investigate
Hello! New Friend.

Goodbye Take Care

We have lived with
life's best dividend,
            our children
But just long enough
to get them ready to go away
To leave us
To be persons
            away from us
            away from our
            special umbrellas
We prepare them
But who prepares us?
To see them only when
they come home to visit.
I think I hate that
I hate the whole idea of
cherished independence
I would like them
near me
            until they find
those partners that might put them
under their own special umbrellas
to keep them safe

But I am selfish
　　　old fashioned
　　　and a fool
And this minute the thought that
they will soon fly away is too
much for me
Oh! my God
　　　I just saw them
　　　walking out the
　　　door.
　　　　　Oy! Gevalt
Goodbye Take Care

Things

There are all kinds of ways
to lose oneself
    there's TM
    (I never know what to
    meditate about, and if
    I ever think about what
    I am trying to avoid
    I won't make it 'til Tuesday)
And
Biofeedback (that's got wires)
EST (how smart they are)
Yoga—supposed to
    be good for sex, all those positions—
    but everyone looks so pure
    (its tough to
    do yoga in
    the A.M.
    and
    come home to
    a dirty kitchen)
Gestalt (very German)
Freud (anti-women)
Modern combinations (madness)
Primal (hard on the throat)
Group (dull-dull)
Conjoin (boring)

Berne's games (when you stop playing
        whadaya do then)
Self realization (too simple)
3 H's (Happy Healthy Holy)
protein only
        (powder naturally
        to get rid of feelings
        of anger and hostility)
Sensuality (you gotta have it)
Bi-sensuality (even better)
Abstinence (impossible)
Fasting (even worse)
Body cleansing (OK)
Gravitation exercises (you gotta understand it)
Group sex (gotta have a group)
        my God, a hundred
        ways to lose
        yourself and start again
With what, please?
        With yourself,
        poorer
        thinner
        and cleaner
        and confused
No more junk foods
or junk thoughts

A higher level
     Yes!
But my question
remains
If you are on a
     higher level
     and your environment
     stays the same
What does your
     higher level do?
     It makes you feel
     awful that's what
And if you were
trying to cope
     with the help
     of pills—
     and now they've
     all been cast aside
     (bad bad pills)
     in favor of looking
     at life
     alert
     awake, no longer
     drugged,
It's an awful trauma—
I have decided to
regress

To go back to
junk everything
and face the world
          slightly drugged with
          a feeling of euphoria
Not thinking about
anything
          Hoping tomorrow
          will be better
I'm going back to smoking
with the threat of cancer
and allied diseases
Reality can kill
          you faster than anything

Addenda
          My seven-year-old just
          threw out all of my pills
As a token of her love
          And my son has
          put a ban on smoking
          in the house
          Couldn't you just
die?

Dick

I saw you
    young
    blond
    tall—handsome and
Aryan
    I was frightened—
    and charmed too!
    As the years passed
    since that seamy elevator
      on 46th Street years ago
Our backgrounds so different
Your parents different from mine
    Catholic
We became friends
You showed me a new way of
    laughing at life
And in my deep heart
I often wonder if things had been different
    What might have been
Your talent has always
    amazed me, and so have you
You have sometimes changed
    my whole day—with a
      special cymbidium just
      for me—you are no longer
      Aryan—
We are the same

Salek

Old
Shy really
Sitting
       talking to a banker
As I watched him
It seemed
       seconds had passed
       when he'd sat talking
         not shy
       to statesmen
       men of literature
       men of power
He was younger
He had confidence
       but
He still had all his papers
in a plain rubber band
There were flashes today of the frightened
young immigrant, who could not speak the language
       all earnest
       trying to please
I could hardly keep my eyes from tearing

Watching
      just looking at him
All of what he owned
      and owed
All of what he had
      fought so hard
to keep—
      All he had come with—
      and all he would leave
      All of it—all of it
         in a plain rubber band

Cologne?

Our survival of this time—my god!
15 years—is more than a puzzlement
It is a combination
of everything
It is our eternal war with life
Parents ill
Children
who
need
us
both
With disappointment and success we took
hands for reasons each of us cannot
remember
We have come through life's war
Is that love?
or endurance
What is marriage anyway?
I don't know
Is it a time to merely partner one's problems?
Even apart we have been together

We should have ended
years ago
      Everyone said so
      they still do
      maybe we'll surprise
      ourselves and last
      wouldn't that be a
      miracle
But then
      this whole trip is one big
      mirage—and we're still
      traveling, aren't we?
        It could be that I like
        your cologne

Where Do I Come From?

For Edith

I come from 5,000 years of ethics
I come from pogroms and ovens
    where my murderers
    charted and graphed
    my death scenes
I am a survivor
I come knowing you don't want me
I come knowing I will make you need me
    I am a Jew
If you let me I can show you who I am
If you kill me something of me will survive
Without me
You have emptiness
    Then there is no ethic
    I did not choose
    to be what I am
But no matter
I have survived it all
    And you
    have you survived your guilt?
Or is there nothing in you that cries
    for what you have done
You must take a lesson from me—
    I never forget
It is part of what I am
    I am a survivor
    I am a Jew

Rain

The best days are
  the ones when
  it rains outside
And inside you
  it's all warm
The rain, God's special surprise,
  lets me think
  of things
   Seeing New York for
   the first time
    A rainy cold Sunday
   And the stores
    all asleep
    gray, the streets quiet
   Steam coming off the roofs
    out of small restaurants
    couples sat, drinking
    talking
    looking at the city
  And the first time I
  said goodbye to Daddy
   Dearborn Station
   Chicago
   The rain pounding on the windows
   of that train
And my silly plaid coat wet with my tears

The him that was once
lost to the rains—that night in Paris
   the walk we had
   after we decided to love one another
   That first time, raining on the beach
  That forever rain the night
  my son was born to
Such a long vigil and
   The morning rain
  my daughter was born in
  It rained for days
  I used to tell my children
  rain was the time God was crying
  I know now that when He looks at the
  children of the world
  They must be
    tears of
      happiness
Why else
would everything good
   happen when it rains?
Rain is the whole world renewing itself
   starting again
   trying just once more
That's the story of
my life
Trying just once more

Sheila

Imagine
Looking like East Hampton
   and coming from Brooklyn
Maybe she should have been Maya Plisetskaya
She seems all alone
The world too big for her to swallow
She is my friend
I want to help. I try
Maybe life is easier when we're less dreamlike
   and accept things as they are
Maybe it helps to know husbands don't change
That children grow up and go away
I always wanted to be willowy—no, it's better to be
   a truck
I roll easier
Sheila, Sheila, look around you
We never know our blessings 'til they've gone away
You might find another willow and intertwine
But you won't if you don't know how beautiful
   you bloom

Suicide

I love the rain
I love the theatre and its forever magic
I love being warm, and needed, and loved
I love my children, and the look of them asleep, all secure
I love the sounds of the mornings, and my father's walk
    coming up the steps with his hard thump, and the *sound of*
    the rattling of packages
I love feeling high on my own energy
Excited about a dress, or a party, or a place
It's good to have friends who really, really care
    whether they approve or not, they care
I like brains, and beauty, and guts.
I don't know about the love of a man . . . I like it . . . But I've
    been so disappointed, I don't know how I feel
I like anticipation, and humor, and performance, and old
    movies, and new dreams
I bless my mother for giving me the energy to keep fighting
    in myself what could depress rather than make me go.

I hate suicide
it's so gutless
I hate giving up or giving in—or selling out
I loathe compromise, and ignorance, and inflexibility
I don't know if it's a Jewish ethic or my own
    But a way of living that tells me one's own way must be
    the way.
There is none other for me.
It's better to be alive than dead
It's better to suffer and struggle and be in pain than give up
For 5000 years Jews were told to give up and somehow they
    didn't, or couldn't, or wouldn't, and they endured
And there is pain, and struggle,
But there is life
And life we can go with
and do
and be
or try
Why not live just for the sake of living
                        Good Morning

Nothing

I wanted you to make tonight something I would
long remember and tuck in the back of my eyes
when I thought of you
You seemed exactly what I had waited so long for
You were going to kiss away my fear
and I was going to be
       young and pretty
       all over again   you were all new
We tried
       and something happened
       The way you looked at
         me
       No, you never looked at me
         You never saw who I was
I was just one more you had found and conquered
       But even that didn't happen
       Was it because I was as a child, or that you
       could not free yourself to hold me?
       It doesn't matter—nothing does—
So here I am, foolish,
       Lonely once again

Camp

I have grown a man
        A boy no longer
        No more burps
        Nor fear of the
        dark—
        Our voices need
            not cross
        tho' I miss your
            voice
This is the beginning
    of goodbye
I have tried
I have given all
I know—and most
I hope you'll never
        need
            You are yourself
            your road is
            your own
            clear
            and ahead
As I stand watching
        you go
The time has come
        too soon

The time has gone
        too fast
    Is 12 so big?
    Is 12 a man?
Yes! my son you
are on your
        way—alone
        Secure
    Straight
I have grown myself a man
    Goodbye—
    I could die

Group Therapy

Group anything has got to be awful
I went to a super group therapy group. I mean it
was so super I had to wait three months to get in.
The doctor, who looked like a huge myna bird, was the
head of everything. He had been trained everywhere.
And each person was hand picked by sex,
style or neurosis.
The room was so perfect—the set from
Lady in the Dark—only better.
After telling our names—first only—the group asked
What we were thinking
            I said
                Spin the bottle
                And an English muffin!
aha. aha he said—deep anxiety. Obviously post-
natal depression brought on by a need for dependency on
your mother. (Are you ready for that?)
The other people had swell ones like murder—homosexuality
or parental approval, distrust or paranoia.

It's true my marriage was in a lot of trouble
My son was too smart and most unusual
My daughter is a Jewish princess
—but these people;
They were really sick
They didn't see the sky or the clouds or life
They didn't even laugh
What a waste of time.
Unless I were reborn a Nordic saint they couldn't help
my madness
No . . . I think I'll keep my madness.

No one else wants it.
Maybe we should have played spin the bottle.

Theatre

Moss Hart said
    "It was the fantasy
    of the unhappy child"
Then what has the happy child?
Any better
or more rewarding
being on it?
    In it
    or going to it?
The happy child—
Hurray for him
He has none of those yearnings,
That damn stage
    makes you feel
    and forget
    who you are, and you lose
    yourself, you become someone else
I always thought
to stand on a proscenium
and spout words
of Williams or Chekhov
was a miracle

And those people—
My kind—the best kind
Forever children
    really
It's like
    being with a "band of angels"
    who somehow are alike
The play is the thing
It's that secure
insecure feeling
    to go at 8:00 somewhere—and find that you belong.
Your other life
    is away from you

For a moment in your life
    you too can forget
    who you are!
And we are both blessed

Who Am I?

I always thought I was
                big and dark
        until reality's mirror
        showed me I was small
                and not dark at all
        Without the cosmetic bottle
        I would be but flush red!
I have always made my face
a porcelain shell
                when really I am one big freckle
forever hiding my spots under
                big hats
                and creams
                and darkened rooms
Those who knew me
                when,
                and see me now
                say to others
                in whispers
                        "she" looked—
not how "she" was or is.

        I am now what I
am expected to be
                porcelainized
                and dark

With only small glimpses
of age to disturb my
pictured sameness
My red mouth
     everpresent
So friends who do not look for age
remember me as I was
And do not notice
     my soul too frightened
     for my mouth
     to change

why am I what I think
I should be
And not what life's mirror
tells me that I am?
Is it because I yearn to please
     those whose years
     cannot be hidden?
And those whose time sits not
too kindly with them?
Or is it for myself?
The never ending riddle
     of what is or what was or if it ever was really
I cannot remember.

I must stay the clock
As long as it will
give me space to
move its hands
Now or before
        back then
            or
        tomorrow
I will sleep quickly
remembering I must be
            who I am
            tomorrow
            Someone could see
            me—and not
            know me—
                and I would
                be alone—
            without even
            today for
            company.

Maybe Tomorrow

I wanted to run away today
    Just not think about
    The market!
    or
    The kids!
    or
    Anything
I wanted to go on this
cold gray day
    and sit on the beach
    with someone
    And I called
    all the someones I knew
    and
    everyone was out
    too busy
They didn't really want to
    They too
    "had too much to do"
Why do we have so much to do
that we never do what we really want
    Is that grown up?
    And responsible?
What fool said
    "It's better to be responsible"

Maybe in my silliness
        I thought
        I could be responsible when I wanted
And then when I didn't
        run away
Now I'm getting like the others
Am I not also responsible
        for my own joy?
                I only wanted to run away for today
                But now the clock says
                it's too late
Time to pick up
Time to be a mommy again
The time for me is over
        for now
Maybe tomorrow
        "No!"
Tomorrow I've got too much to do
        There I go
        again
        Plans that I made for me
        Gone—away
Have I lost anything
Really?

Depressed

Sad, sad,
But not depressed
What does that mean?
My face does not wear a tragic mask
(Almost never)
But it wears one!
I walk with such speed
You would think I was a track star.
I do all of my errands—and
Wash my hair every day.
I have a positive philosophy
I tell everyone to cheer up . . .
I don't smoke, drink,
Or compulsively eat
Except at 3:00 A.M., when no one is looking.
My skin is free of acne,
My breath is hermetically sealed—I use Binaca daily.
My hair is the latest
Dyed, and cut just right
I smile . . .
Sad, sad, but not depressed.
Now, what does that mean?
It means—it means—I'm dying,
But my mask is on—is yours?

No No's

My Mother
       is not just a Mother
            tho' that would be enough—
My Mother
       is a woman of courage
My Mother
            has strength
            She is the American flag
            independent
            forever hopeful
            like no other. She is proud
                 I am her daughter
                 and
I am just lucky that I have known her.
            Without her
I would understand no.
            Knowing her
There are No No's
only try again
It could be that she would have been
a lampshade if she understood can't
            Marvelous for me
                 she cannot!

Thursday

We stole hours
to be together midweek.
    We stopped at a
    plant shop on the highway.
An odd soup bowl said
to me "take me home"
And you bought it for me
We looked at a
fountain, the kind I
    had as a child
And a funny statue
was spouting water
        into ivy—oh! to
        feel 12 again.
            There was a big
            table—filled
            with sea
            shells
                You tried
to kiss me near the
pots—and I wanted
you to stop—or
didn't I—we have
        never had a day
like today
not in a long time

The kiss in the back of the
          nursery made me
          feel uncomfortable.
          16 years, and
          I was shy?
Marriage and daily
life have really
done a number on
us, haven't they?
Just think how in love
we could be if we ever
pursued it
          But we seem
to want to recapture
something today
          in the woodsy
restaurant where I'd been
a thousand years ago.
We felt warm didn't we?
We were trying for instant romance.
          I noticed there
weren't any married couples
I could just tell
You said all the right things

The ocean so
glorious like
silver blue lamé   .
          And suddenly
          you kissed me
And I liked it
          But then I
          noticed the clock
          Our time was up, the
          vodka had just begun
          to work.
Was it that or
          us?
Or the ocean?
          Never mind
I was sorry as I looked at you
          that we've
wasted so much time fighting and
          not caring
There is still something
special about you—
          Something odd like the
          pot that asked me to
          take it home
              Take me home—now
                  Please!

Mother's Day

Mother's Day is supposed to be the day my children honor me.
How stupid, how wrong. It is I who should honor them
That I have been allowed by some biological system to give
birth—to give life, the greatest gift of all. There is
no more need for gifts!

Being a Mother allows me to love with complete
selfishness. And a good reason to care for
myself.
      They have given me joy
      They have given me pain
      They give me a chance at immortality . . .
      what more . . . what more
Motherhood is not always glorious. It is boring and tedious,
and a thief of my heart, and my time.
It gives me a right to worry, grieve, scream, holler, mold,
    swear,
laugh, hate, wonder.
It gives me another childhood.
I hope they'll grow up and really like me.

I have
Two people I really adore—and what a gift that is.
We didn't choose each other but I think
we're making it work.
      I hope so
      I think I'm going to cry.
      Mothers are supposed to.
         For Shepsie
         And Lisa Beth
            Mother's Day '77

Father's Day

Tonight as you sat
    on the round tweed chair
your legs weary with age
It crossed my mind
how young and handsome
    sitting at your big desk, making deals
    you were. So strong. How cruel is time
    How terrible is age.

I see a young man—
    black curly hair, wet with the
    sweat of work, filled with dreams
    of American success

As you got your success
    and the years went by and hair
    whitened, I never saw you
    age. I see it only for a moment
    or two now, and when I do
    I hate it

Time is my enemy
Time is my thief

But time cannot steal the
        Pictures in my head
        indelible forever
        you are still filled with
        incredible dreams and
        for some moments, strong with
        energy, and when
        I see that
            I forget time
            I forget my enemy
            Time is my friend

The clock has stopped
and you are—you again
I wonder today, knowing what
you always do for me
if I have ever done
anything for you, really.

Don't tell me if I haven't.
I couldn't stand it—I
don't have the time!

Women's Lib–Yes or No

Why do we need a movement to prove our worth?
Why do we need lectures, to prove that we know
      what we are?
We are not men
We are women
We do what we do
You do what you do
If we need to work
      You need to pay us our due
If we bear you children
      You need to help us
If you leave us, and we are alone with our children
      We can help ourselves if we must.
There is a place for you
There is a place for us
We are not slaves
Neither are you
We are equal
We each have a place
We ask that you are just
      That you give us our due
Some of us know this
Most of you don't
Some of us feel you trap us
If we let you it is our fault

We are not slaves
Neither are you
We have a need for a home
Maybe you do or do not
If we cannot be together
You may go your own way
            You are the child of a mother too
I will not hold you
But you cannot ask me to love you
            if you leave me
                to be alone.
Then I am both of us
I am woman and I am man too!
            And that is not my way.
But I will be
If I have to be
I can be anything
I ask no more than what is due me
            I need you, I do
                I am a woman

Television

Do you know when I was a little girl
I didn't watch television
         because there wasn't any
         We had radio—and music
         and "the movies"
         and families
         We had causes—
         and singing
             And no one I
knew was divorced
         or o.d.'d
         or ran away
         or did anything
             except be
             what they were
                 expected to be
There were real heros
         and school
         and plays
         and lessons
             But mostly families
We grew up but then
it wasn't correct to
         expect anything because they had
         the right to do and be what they
         wanted

And they had grown differently
    Because when you
    were a tiny person
    no one watched television
        And now
        it's taken the place of
            company
            manners and families
            good looks
            breeding
            knowledge
            reading
            music
            imagination
It's taken care of all of that
with a big screen
            and color and
            sound
        And easy
            and at home
            and . . . So Boring
No one I knew
        went to jail
        had a drug problem
        or "shrunk" every day

No one did anything they
weren't expected to do
    And then
    we began growing up
      and we saw everything
    we loved it
      And then somehow
    everyone knew everything
      And you were lucky
      if you weren't divorced
      if your kids didn't o.d.
No! I'm saving television
for my very
    very
    old
    age
When I'm too infirm
to care about anything
else—or maybe
by that time I'll
be dead—and I won't care
Especially
what everyone's missed
    by forever watching television
    Whatever happened to
      Families?

Yellow Roses

Bar Harbor is cold!
It was summer
I was young, young
They said Sweep the stage, paint the scenery, be an actress
This is stock
This is experience
This is life
I was young, young

The accident—like a movie
They said, Do you know the lines
I don't know . . . I called home . . . And told them
3000 miles away. He hopped a plane to N.Y.
Got dumped in St. Louis. Another plane to Boston
A florist in Boston sold yellow roses
A cab to Bar Harbor, another to Surrey, Maine
He was tired
I was very, very young
I walked onto the stage
I saw him.
all huge and dark and beaming, the roses wilting, my heart
leaping, the play over, the curtain down

He saw me
He saw me
He made it
He came
He cared
I cried!
I was an actress.
Someone gave me roses
Someone cared

This is stock
This is experience
    And he has always, always made it
    No matter what
    My Father.
      Thank You,
      Daddy

      The
      Roses
      Have
      Never
      Wilted